A Bees' Difficult Search for Food

by Mary Ellen Klukow

Illustrated by Romina Martí

About the Author

After earning her B.S. in Wildlife and Conservation Biology from Ohio University, Mary Ellen Klukow spent the first few years of her career in environmental research. She is now proud and happy to share her knowledge with young readers.

About the Illustrator

Romina Martí is an illustrator who lives and works in Barcelona, Spain, where her ideas come to life for all audiences. She loves to discover and draw all kinds of creatures from around the planet, who then become the main characters for the majority of her work. To learn more, go to: rominamarti.com

AMICUS ILLUSTRATED and AMICUS INK are published by Amicus
P.O. Box 1329, Mankato, MN 56002
www.amicuspublishing.us

LIBRARY OF CONGRESS CATALOGING-IN-PUBLICATION DATA
Names: Klukow, Mary Ellen, author. | Martí, Romina, illustrator.
Title: A bee's difficult search for food / by Mary Ellen Klukow; illustrated by Romina Martí.
Description: Mankato, Minnesota : Amicus/Amicus Ink, [2020] | Series: Animal habitats at risk | Audience: K to grade 3. | Includes bibliographical references.
Identifiers: LCCN 2018047578 (print) | LCCN 2018048864 (ebook) | ISBN 9781681517858 (pdf) | ISBN 9781681517032 (library binding) | ISBN 9781681524894 (pbk.)
Subjects: LCSH: Bumblebees—Behavior—Juvenile literature. | Bumblebees—Conservation—Juvenile literature. | Habitat conservation—Juvenile literature.
Classification: LCC QL568.A6 (ebook) | LCC QL568.A6 K58 2020 (print) | DDC 595.79/9—dc23
LC record available at https://lccn.loc.gov/2018047578

EDITOR: Wendy Dieker
DESIGNER: Kathleen Petelinsek

Printed in the United States of America
HC 10 9 8 7 6 5 4 3 2 1
PB 10 9 8 7 6 5 4 3 2 1

A rusty patched bumblebee climbs to the entrance of her hive. She is a scout. Her job is to find flowers for her family. They will eat nectar and pollen from the flowers.

The hive is in a hole under the grass. There, worker bees tend the queen and her eggs. Buzz, buzz.

The scout starts to fly toward a field she remembers.
Last year it was full of yummy wildflowers.

When she lands, she doesn't recognize the field. The grass and flowers are gone. The field has been turned into a neighborhood.

The bee can't find any food here. She needs flowers. But what's that over there?

Dandelions! Dandelions are an important source of food for bees. She buzzes over quickly, ready to eat. But suddenly, a cloud of chemicals comes out of a sprayer! A landscaper thinks these flowers are weeds. He wants those flowers gone.

The scout flies to a flowerpot near a house. Before she can gather any pollen, she hears, "Oh, no! A bee!" A woman swats at her, trying to kill her. Most people are scared of bees. They don't know that bees don't sting unless they are scared. This isn't a safe spot to find food.

A long time ago, finding new fields was easy. Flowers were everywhere. But now, the scout bee flies over concrete and buildings. She searches and searches. Where are the flowers?

The bee is starting to lose energy, but then she spots something! Just ahead, there is a big garden of fruit and vegetable plants. It even has native wildflowers! She dives down. She aims for a big flower and lands in a cloud of pollen.

Still dusted with pollen, she gathers nectar. Then she hops to another flower and gathers some more nectar. Every time she lands on a new flower, she pollinates it.

Flowers that have been pollinated
will grow fruit and veggies. Now
the gardener will have lots of food!

Once she is full, she heads home. When she arrives, bees from all over the hive crowd around her. Then she starts to do a waggle dance. She wiggles and circles and turns. This is how she tells the other bees where the flowers are.

The bees fly off to gather food. This hive was lucky. All over the world, though, animals that pollinate flowers are dying.

If we don't feed these insects, they won't be around to pollinate the plants to grow our fruits and vegetables. They need our help.

Where Rusty Patched Bumblebees Live

Rusty patched bumblebees live in small areas around the Great Lakes and Eastern regions of the United States.

KEY

Rusty patched bumblebee range

Pollinators at Risk

Animals that pollinate plants help fruits and vegetables grow. Without pollinators, we wouldn't have food like apples, squash, cucumbers, or even chocolate! Rusty patched bumblebees aren't the only animals that pollinate plants, and they're not the only pollinators that are in danger. Butterflies, moths, wasps, even bats and birds are all struggling with lost habitats. Many government agencies and concerned citizens are helping by protecting pollinator habitats from mowing or chemicals.

You can save bees!

- Plant native wildflowers! Bees from all over will come to drink nectar from them.
- Don't use bug sprays or weed killers in the garden. These can kill bees.
- Don't squish bees! They won't sting you if you don't bother them.

Glossary

landscaper A person who designs and takes care of the lawn, trees, and other plants around houses and other buildings.

native Living naturally in a certain area.

nectar A sugary fluid that plants make; bees use it to make honey.

pollen A fine powder that plants make; it is used to make the seeds inside fruits and vegetables.

pollinate To gather pollen from one plant and leave it on another so that it can create seeds.

scout A worker bee that finds new food sources.

waggle dance The movements a scout bee does to tell other worker bees how to travel to a new food source.

Websites

DK Find Out!: Endangered Animals
https://www.dkfindout.com/us/more-find-out/special-events/endangered-animals/
Learn more about endangered animals and the threats they face.

Kids Growing Strong: Pollinators
https://kidsgrowingstrong.org/pollinators/
Bees aren't the only animals that can pollinate. Learn about other pollinators!

National Geographic Kids: Mission Animal Rescue – Raise Awareness!
https://kids.nationalgeographic.com/explore/nature/mission-animal-rescue/raise-awareness/
Discover even more ways to help save endangered animals!

Every effort has been made to ensure that these websites are appropriate for children. However, because of the nature of the Internet, it is impossible to guarantee that these sites will remain active indefinitely or that their contents will not be altered.

Read More

Bath, Louella. *Saving Endangered Animals.* New York: PowerKids Press, 2017.

Raum, Elizabeth. *Bees Build Beehives.* Mankato, Minn.: Amicus, 2018.

Stark, Kristy. *Honeybees.* Huntington Beach, Calif.: Teacher Created Materials, 2018.